Young cat! If you keep
your eyes open enough,
oh, the stuff you will learn!
The most wonderful stuff!
　　—*I Can Read with My Eyes Shut!*

Seuss-isms for Success

Insider Tips on Economic Health from the

GOOD DOCTOR

Introduction by

TOM PETERS

Random House New York

TM and © 1999 by Dr. Seuss Enterprises, L.P.
Introduction © 1999 Tom Peters–Excel/A California Partnership.
All rights reserved under International and Pan-American Copyright Conventions.
Published in the United States by Random House, Inc., New York, and
simultaneously in Canada by Random House of Canada Limited, Toronto.
www.randomhouse.com/seussville
ISBN: 0-679-89477-2   Library of Congress Catalog Card Number: 98-67043
Printed in the United States of America   10 9 8 7 6 5 4 3 2 1

I've had a problem with the "spirituality movement" in business.

Business is not a religion. (No matter what the Wall Street types say!) But I do consider myself charter member #1 in the "spirited movement."

Which is why I want to endorse this book. And heartily recommend it.

Business can be shabby. And demeaning to the individual. And tragicomic. Look at how we all identify with Dilbert's days of rage.

But business can also be inspiring! Creating cool stuff that millions of people fall in love with—from supersonic aircraft to Post-its and Ziploc bags and Velcro and Magic Markers.

Business means pushing paper. And filling out forms. And people shouting at other people in frustration. But while we get irritated at flight delays and lost luggage, we also enjoy the business-made miracle of planes with millions of parts getting us safely and rapidly home from school for the holidays and on time to a best friend's wedding 1,800 miles from home...tomorrow.

Business, then, is life. For worst. And for better. The endless meetings. The tons of paperwork. The bruised egos and lack of appreciation. And: the romance of the new. The chance for growth and travel and exotic association with exotic people.

Since business is life, who better to guide and amuse us than Dr. Seuss!

TOM PETERS
September 1998

Congratulations!
Today is your day.
You're off to Great Places!
You're off and away!

You have brains in your head.
You have feet in your shoes.
You can steer yourself
any direction you choose.
—*Oh, the Places You'll Go!*

On micromanagement

Oh, the jobs people work at!
Out west, near Hawtch-Hawtch,
there's a Hawtch-Hawtcher Bee-Watcher.
His job is to watch...
is to keep both his eyes on the lazy town bee.
A bee that is watched will work harder, you see.

Well...he watched and he watched.
But, in spite of his watch,
that bee didn't work any harder. Not mawtch.

And poor Mr. Potter,
T-crosser,
I-dotter.
He has to cross *t*'s
and he has to dot *i*'s
in an I-and-T factory
out in Van Nuys!

—*Did I Ever Tell You How Lucky You Are?*

On growth

I laughed at the Lorax, "You poor stupid guy!
You never can tell what some people will buy."

Business is business!
And business must grow
regardless of crummies in tummies, you know.

—The Lorax

On surpassing the competition

You can do three,
but I can do more.
You have three,
but I have four.

—Ten Apples Up on Top!

On cycles

You won't lag behind,
    because you'll have the speed.
You'll pass the whole gang
    and you'll soon take the lead.

Except when you *don't*.
Because, sometimes, you *won't*.
    —*Oh, the Places You'll Go!*

On speculation

"Young man," laughed the farmer,
"You're sort of a fool!
You'll *never* catch fish
In McElligot's Pool!"

"Hmmm..." answered Marco,
"It *may* be you're right.
I've been here three hours
Without one single bite.
There *might* be no fish...
...But, again,
Well, there *might*!"

If I wait long enough; if I'm patient and cool,
Who knows *what* I'll catch in McElligot's Pool!

—*McElligot's Pool*

A simple thimble *could* cost less
than a single shingle would, I guess.
So I think that the single shingle *should*
cost more than the simple thimble would.
—*Oh Say Can You Say?*

On chaos theory
They only could say it just
"happened to happen" and was
not very likely to happen again.
—*The 500 Hats of Bartholomew Cubbins*

On trusting your instincts
I was following a Nowhere Hunch,
a real dumb thing to do!
Everybody sometimes does it.
Even me. And even you.

Oh, you get so many hunches
that you don't know ever quite
if the right hunch is a wrong hunch!
Then the wrong hunch might be right!

—*Hunches in Bunches*

On the stock market
The storm starts
when the drops start dropping.
When the drops stop dropping
then the storm starts stopping.
—*Oh Say Can You Say?*

On business trips

More easy to pack than a suitcase or grip,
Those horns carry all that he needs on a trip:
A thread and a needle for mending his socks,
His tooth brush,
A cup,
And two three-handed clocks.
And his velvet umbrella,
His vegetable chopper,
And also his gold-plated popping-corn popper
And a grasshopper cage
for his favorite grass hopper.

—On Beyond Zebra!

…your Grox must be packed
and locked up in a Grox Box,
which costs much, much more
than a little old fox box.
So it's heaps a lot cheaper
to fly with your foxes
than waste all that money
on boxes for Groxes.

—Oh Say Can You Say?

On maintaining a competitive edge

So, on beyond Z!
It's high time you were shown
That you really *don't* know
all there is to be known.
—*On Beyond Zebra!*

You have to be smart
and keep watching their feet.
Because sometimes they stand
on their tiptoes and cheat.
—*Happy Birthday to You!*

They will get them
if we let them.
Come! We can not
let them get them.
—*Ten Apples Up on Top!*

So I said to myself,
   "Now, I'll just have to start
To be twice as careful
   and be twice as smart.
I'll watch out for trouble
   in front and back sections
By aiming my eyeballs
   in different directions."
   —*I Had Trouble in Getting to Solla Sollew*

On synergy

Fritz needs Fred and Fred needs Fritz.
Fritz feeds Fred and Fred feeds Fritz.
Fred feeds Fritz with ritzy Fred food.
Fritz feeds Fred with ritzy Fritz food.
And Fritz, when fed, has often said,
"I'm a Fred-fed Fritz.
Fred's a Fritz-fed Fred."
—*Oh Say Can You Say?*

On delegating

Sighed Mayzie, a lazy bird
   hatching an egg:
"I'm tired and I'm bored
And I've kinks in my leg
From sitting, just sitting here
   day after day.
It's *work!* How I hate it!
I'd *much* rather play!
I'd take a vacation, fly off for a rest
If I could find *someone* to stay on my nest!
If I could find someone, I'd fly away—free...."
Then Horton, the Elephant, passed by her tree.

—*Horton Hatches the Egg*

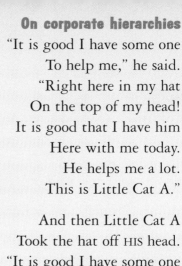

On corporate hierarchies

"It is good I have some one
To help me," he said.
"Right here in my hat
On the top of my head!
It is good that I have him
Here with me today.
He helps me a lot.
This is Little Cat A."

And then Little Cat A
Took the hat off HIS head.
"It is good I have some one
To help ME," he said.
"This is Little Cat B.
And I keep him about,
And when I need help
Then I let him come out."

—*The Cat in the Hat*
Comes Back

On downsizing
The time has come.
The time is now.
Just go.
Go.
GO!
I don't care how.

Marvin K. Mooney!
Don't you know
the time has come
to go, Go, GO!

—*Marvin K. Mooney Will You Please Go Now!*

On innovation

And ZATZ is the letter
I use to spell Zatz-it
Whose nose is so high
that 'most nobody pats it...
So, to get there and do it,
I built an invention:
The Three-Seater Zatz-it
Nose-Patting Extension.
—*On Beyond Zebra!*

The places I hiked to!
The roads that I rambled
To find the best eggs
that have ever been scrambled!
If you want to get eggs
you can't buy at a store,
You have to do things
never thought of before.
—*Scrambled Eggs Super!*

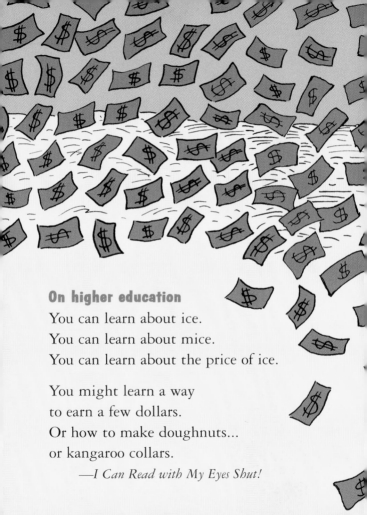

On higher education

You can learn about ice.
You can learn about mice.
You can learn about the price of ice.

You might learn a way
to earn a few dollars.
Or how to make doughnuts...
or kangaroo collars.

— *I Can Read with My Eyes Shut!*

SO...
that's why I tell you
to keep your eyes wide.
To keep them wide open...
at least on one side.

—*I Can Read with My Eyes Shut!*